Sacred, Secret, and Holy

Original Prose

By: karnes

May love find us all.

-karnes

I am yours now, forever, until my eyes reflect death itself.

I will go and let hunger take me over. You were always a talker and I had been too used to silence before. My ears were nothing more than a body part that did not work properly. They only caught what was told behind my back.

You are everything sacred, secret, and holy.

The world around us may be burning and eating itself, but we are the ones who are seeing life happen with wide eyes. There is still love outside of the flames. There is still a magical touch given to angels fleeing hell.

I am aware of your moons. I am aware of the energy you consume me with. You may end up drowning me in my own body with the way you push and pull my tides. I will never give up trying to reach you. Even if my breath becomes the wind, I will come running to you.

Maybe I have too much hatred and resentment in my heart to love again. Maybe my soul is too heavy for anyone to hold up and care for. My self-loathing is at an all-time high, and I apologize to anyone who has had to deal with my insides. I am tired. I am lonely. I am scared I will never brave this pain. Maybe a miracle will find me before my face erodes again.

I can see happiness exuding out of you. I know I helped you get there, but that's where it stops. My job was to get you out of the life you were scared to leave. Now look at how you are flying. I will stand back and watch, but love left the day you said you did not need me the way I needed you.

I know one day distance will only be a relationship based on the location of sour souls. We are separated now, but time catches up to everyone if you chase after a love you want. I have found you, and there is no turning back to see what I have missed. It is just you and me. That is the only vision needed for me to see how much I love missing you.

We have not had our time yet, but life is an extraordinary thing once you find someone to share your stories with. Someone who is brave enough to conquer a darkness you have lived in for years to become a better light. Finding you, I have found how wings can be made for comfort, instead of only used by some to crash midflight.

Love is what happens when two souls escape the flesh long enough to be married in the stars. Their return home is the essence. Their return home to the human side of life is the product of revered promises kept safe by kissing whatever hurts after.

I am scared you do not want me the same. That you are better at being alone than you are with my hands around your body and heart. That you have been alone too long for anyone to tell you how much love they have for you. Your roots are too deep for me to nurture, to water without flooding your insides.

Pressing finger to thumb, a star is pulled down for you. Where the earth speaks and flowers remain at rest, you will find my love for you. I am closer to a life without you than with you. But love conquers all of us once we release our hearts back into the wild.

I have been here long enough to know the difference between someone wanting your soul and someone wanting only your attention. Give yourself to those who never make you question your place in their lives. We only get one of them, so make sure you choose wisely who you spend your breaths on.

I want a life that can hold me when my arms forget how to hold myself. I want a heart that is true and understanding when my own becomes weak and unable to protect my soul. I am exhausted of pretending I am okay without any love to speak of. Life has never been the same since I forgot about you. I thought it was impossible to remove a limb from your body without dying. Since you have left, I have learned that an amputated heart still beats long after its previous purpose has died.

You never know how alone someone can be until you think you understand how low someone's low really is. My body has shifted with the sun again. My soul has tipped over the moon again. My breathing feels like your hands are over my mouth. The count has made it to ten, but you insist to keep them on me.

My sorrows drag me down, then I hear your laugh and a fullness comes over me. Every color comes from your eyes and life takes on a new meaning. Love is a warmth given off by someone who only has their broken heart to give. At times, it completes all of the pain living within me.

I have been trying to find someone to replace you instead of trying to be happy on my own again. I still have bad days that feel the same as the day you said goodbye. Every time I see you shine now, I know it has nothing to do with me.

You bring out the soul in me when I lose purpose and company. You have always had this way about you that is supernatural, something not born here. You are never far from my thoughts. You are the keeper of everything beautiful and destined for magic. You are a lighthouse resting on the shore of my darkness.

You will be my endless entity. A feeling unlike any other. A woman all of her own energy and power. A crown made from the moon, with her light kept safe inside the thorns. We all come from some place, some forgotten realm. I just want to go back there with you.

I used to watch you sleep. Now I am seeing you leave. Too many nights I kept my eyes open until the sun spoke your name. I wanted you safe. I wanted you to feel and be loved like the flowers are when the rain falls. We still are not that far away, yet, your face looks happier now without me. You are still the love of my life, my journey, my poetry.

Love never leaves us. Regardless of how we feel, my words will be your blues and greens. It is how we are connected; Bones to galaxies. Flesh to constellations. We have always been able to be ourselves. I still feel you now. I still know you are here, so I smile no matter how much it hurts to these days.

When the world sleeps, my dreams take me to you. Love is simply you. I will never think of it differently, but time stops for the lucky ones. We used to be it. Now, I am back to living without you. My next relationship will be the last. She will hold me when my demons grow faces and birth names, fighting for my company. She will win, because she will stay this time.

My wounds will heal. Even on days that feel unbearable. My pain may define the problem, but it won't define me. I am stuck somewhere along the path and journey. I look to my left and right, and I see a light. I see who I will become.

You asked me what I felt. You laughed because you told me I do it for a living. I told you it was the feeling of excitement. It is writing something for someone you never knew could see you. It is showing your soul to another human for the first time, hoping it is a forever kind of way.

Some days I feel more alone than others. It hits me and keeps me company, especially tonight. All I want to do is reach for your body and hold you tightly, instead of this pen writing about my lonely. Maybe one day I will be less of who I was with you and something more for who I am now.

Come to me like early morning shine. Speak to me with love, as if you finally believe in it this time. Wrap me up in your bones, in your home, with no hesitation in your eyes.

You took the words from my mouth and gave them a melody, a feeling, a memorable texture. My life had no sound until your voice made mine break. My life was nothing more than an exit strategy for anyone who ever entered it.

Somebody will come into your life and not make you question if you are good enough. They will show you how much they have missed you. They will stay, because you have always been more than enough to everyone, except those who never knew who they were to begin with. Someone will wake up with such a love and conviction for you each and every day, you will finally feel what it's like to love, when your love is given back to you. I can only hope you see the good in you and what you offer, rather than what others never cared to see.

Life is simple;

Find what you love.

Work at what you love.

Do what you love.

Everything else is bullshit

getting in your way.

Within these broken bones,

the beauty remains free.

The magic is composed of

lullabies and stripped down

tendencies of a lost man looking

for his way back home.

Some escape to leave something behind. I escape to discover something new. There is never a more opportune time to discover a newly given purpose than when you are feeling as lost as the moon is during a stroll in a blue sky. Some things may feel out of place, but you will never feel more like yourself once you understand not everything is where others want it to be. It is where we learn to appreciate them to be and how long it took them to get there.

Lately, there has been a feeling I have tried to articulate.

But when I speak, your name is the only thing that comes out.

It is the only thing I know how to pronounce correctly once the

pain sets in and I need refuge from it all.

If morning comes and tries to take you away from me again, I will wait up before the earth rises and show it how much fight there is left in me. Being without you for this long already, even hell doesn't have a demon strong enough to do such a thing. But I will keep waiting up if it ever does.

It is during this time of watching these colors dance across a sky where you used to be that I remember you most. It is in the dead of winter's delightful goodbye that I know how being alive is only a curse to those who keep December from turning over. I see you everywhere, which if you know me, you know how difficult it has been keeping my eyes closed all this time.

What if I only saw you and you never noticed me? I wonder what life would be like if we missed every opportunity and gave away every chance at what was supposed to be.

I just want to lay with you in bed and know when I look over at you, love has found us both in a moment of vulnerable acceptance. A place where togetherness has no comparison.

Then you realize it is all temporary except for the moments that make you appreciate the memory a little more, a little deeper. Fate can only make love to conviction if you are willing to break your heart a few times in this life.

The moon knows all your secrets. It is there we all live and die. It is there that love keeps its shine. I have been obsessed with unearthly things ever since you became my life. Now that you are gone, I am still in awe of the unexplainable ways life happens to us all when we are too busy dying to notice goodbyes come in waves, instead of the rain.

I feel you the most when our sky turns from blue to red.

Those colors have come to define you and I.

It used to be green and yellow, but the bet we

made turned the devil into more a game of

hide and seek, rather than a lovely serenade

of together and always. For the rest of my

life, I will be chasing after ghosts who once

held my life and love inside of them.

She said, "Why me? It seems like you have so many beautiful women who want your attention."

I laughed, but not too loudly. I did not want her to feel judged for a statement she believed in.

"My attention cannot be had. It has been yours from the beginning. I am already taken, because of you. Even if you tell me you are not always beautiful, my desire for you will never cease. Someone like you isn't supposed to exist in my world. It is why I have never told you. Some beauty if spoken about, tends to leave with the same wings it arrived with."

I am making an effort to strengthen who I am, so maybe one day I can hold someone better than the excuses I am carrying and cannot seem to put down.

When all the stars are dead and gone, your presence, your

shine, your light, will remain steady in glory and grace.

The love is there. I can feel it in my soul. I simply need to let go of a past that has more ghosts than angels. I have kept the door and windows opened, hoping you would find your way back to me. But all I have felt is the wind killing me in the same ways you did before you left; one foot in, one foot out.

We found the devil in the love we made. When we are apart, I am afraid of losing you for good. Tell me where you run to and I will tell you that you are my beginning, my unquestionable start.

I love when you come near me. It is a sacred dance of souls. The leaning and bending. The soft and subtle. It is where we cross over into forever.

I am in love, but I cannot tell my heart that she doesn't need it right now. There is a kind of patience required for certain things I am just now understanding I never had to begin with. It is being able to see then moon, but never getting close enough to feel her light. Some things are meant to be appreciated by distance only.

I am tired of writing about love, so I will sleep with the

darkness for a while and see where the light hits me next.

It is the strangest feeling to love someone who cannot love you back. Your entire being throws up everything it had been told about what love is to us and for us. Once you know who that human is for you, there is no turning back. There is only a lifelong war between holding on and letting go.

Once I get to you, there will be no getting rid of me. Once you find where you finally belong, it is the permanent state of nirvana. It is where all humans hope they end up when the heart decides on what love is and what it is not.

She is someone you will never forget about. It has nothing to do with who she is, but rather what she makes you feel. There is a love inside of her you have never had before. It is what makes and gives these words all the emotions I fail to give myself when I lack the strength to love the love I have for myself. Some days I break wide open. Other days I break from within. Either way, she gives me a backbone to borrow so I can attempt to stand with my emotions.

I wish I knew how to get to you, how to make these feelings I have for you more tangible than words on cotton paper. Maybe when we are supposed to meet, I will be better equipped to handle missing you better than I do now.

I am consumed with you. I swear if I did not know any better, I would believe your words to be the gospel and your love to be the break in every goddamn bone I am made of. It is daunting to say the least, but you have become quite the haunting for me. I thought I was the only ghost living in this house.

If I could, I would marry you, all of you. I want my life to be your life, without forcing anything upon you. I want my steps to be in sync with yours. I want my body to lay horizontally with yours; in life, in death.

She is an easy morning during a winter's day. She is autumn and all its oranges and yellows. There is a deepness to her only mother nature can feel. Take your hands and run them through the wind. It is the only chance you will get to feel her in her fullness, in her laudation.

I take in my breath, hold it against these bones, then let go.

You are only alive once you let in the beauty others never get a chance at knowing.

I am lost to a wild I am consumed by. Where there is love, there is a chance I will always be the one chasing it, even if it never chases me back to the start.

Some may look at me and call me a broken man, but it all depends on what your definition of broken is. My heart may be misplaced at the moment, but it still fucking carries a song no one will ever be able to sing by themselves. Not everyone can understand these notes I am made of. I am thankful for the instrument I have become.

Maybe I wasn't any good for you at the end of us. Maybe I knew you had already left and my efforts were better used at leaving what would never be mine again. You made goodbye look easy to me. Even after my attempt the first time, yours became the only one that kept me from moving on. I sit with my hands in my face, wondering where the next beat of my heart will go and where your heart runs to next.

I write to simply get you back. There is not another reason why it is I do this. Of course, my soul needs to be stretched and then returned to its natural state, but my words, my feelings, this blood, it is only for you.

Lonely knows me better than any friend of mine. It has been there for me through the worst of times, through the best of times. It kisses my wounds and resets my heart. It gives me purpose. It gives me my beginning and ending. Where I am going, it will remain a part of me. A friend, a lover, a known enemy I cannot seem to kill or suffocate any longer.

Love came to me today. It handed me your memory and said be gentle with it all. A love like yours doesn't come around here often. When it leaves, it will be the stepping stone, the skipped rock across the water's mouth I have needed. Love is a lot like leaving, but I cannot let you go.

I am not here to end up without you. I am here to have a place in your life, in your daily remembrance of what it feels like when your lips need to touch mine. I am in need of you in ways you are not used to. When I awake and reach for you, my hands will always go to a different part of your body. I am not an animal looking for scraps. I am a human, dying for some fucking soul, a fire I can devour.

I always end up in someone else's life that doesn't need what I am offering. I fall too fast when the other person has yet to reach the edge. I am trying to understand fully not everyone will want what you have. They may want parts of what makes you the way you are and that's all. My downfall comes when I think they want something more or at least what I do. It is the greatest ache there is when you feel something for someone who doesn't feel it at all. My expectations always outweigh the reality. More times than not, I break my own fucking heart. I will be changing that as I move into a new phase of my life. What's meant to be in your life won't ever ask you to stay. They will keep showing up without telling you. I just need someone who wakes up next to me, feeling what I feel for them. That's all. Maybe I am too simple of a man, but those are the most important parts of life to me.

My words aren't the kind others are used to. It is why I

appreciate those who are here. I do not want to be like

everyone else you read or follow. I want to be a reason why you

are uncomfortable with feeling something you have yet to

explore or have exercised.

I will drown you in flowers if you let me. You deserve to be told often how supreme and immense you are. You deserve to be told how you not only make the sun shine brighter, but you are the sole reason its rays find me on any given day. I am beginning to believe in my scars and why they ended up there in the first place. If you do not know already, I have been yours since you said hello to me. You have been my favorite feeling ever since then. I only know extremes. I never want to breathe without you being the reason why.

Some nights I am afraid of what the light will bring me. Then I roll over on my side to find you fighting off every demon running towards me. Fear is a joke the devil slips into your ear to make you afraid of what was never there to begin with. You keep me steady, a corporeal melody of hums and a slight squeeze of my hand. You take me where I was made broken and love me even more. You are a precious sensation nestled between the fifth and sixth rib. I noticed my smile meant more to me today.

I looked at her and felt something come over me. It was a warm blanket to my ache. It was a calm to the storm I oftentimes can be.

"I haven't missed someone like this in a very long time. I've missed this feeling." Her eyes went straight to mine. Her hands went into my hands. "What feeling is that?" She asked me with such a genuine tone and expression. I leaned in and pressed my heart against hers.

"The feeling of longing, of connection, of missing someone you cannot get enough of. The feeling of wanting to wake up and find that person as soon as possible. The feeling of a home you never knew could house you. The sensation of knowing someone cares."

After that night, lost was nothing more than being somewhere entangled with her.

I applaud those who do not need anyone in their lives to be happy or at peace. I used to be that way. It taught me how much I do need someone else. I am at an age where my solitude isn't what it once was. It is difficult to stay in peace when you are missing someone else. I am living the best life I possibly can and it is the best one I have had in many years. I am ready to settle down with someone, but not settling to satisfy my loneliness. This year has taught and showed me a lot. I have listened and watched closely. I am ready.

There is a love set out before me. Hands of grace touch my leather face with intentions to set me free. You have always been a distant embrace, a storied promise to the man I can be at times. Love made me this way. It has never fully accepted my truth, but not many can if I am being honest. If I am to ever find love again, I will go where it asks me to. You are my darling, my sweet conviction of dream and memory. Wherever you go, the sea and I will never be too far behind. The moon you baby and carry with your shifting moods, provides me a glimpse of your miraculous and victorious way of being a holy thing. Love is what made me, but you have been what's kept me from dying.

There are days I am still trying to find words to say to you that would make you stay. I am not who I was before you. I am no longer searching for love itself. I am after something simple, something less fragile than the bomb I ingurgitated to keep everyone else safe. My life is not in need of anyone. I am in need of a feeling that keeps escaping me.

Let my love be the last thing that leaves me. May there be more left to give back to you once these bones have given way to the soul. Strike your match and leave me there to burn. Please, my love, do not worry for me. I was born already ablaze and set to smolder in these ashes of who we were.

You are worthy of a life, a love, a feeling of utter and complete rapture. I hope you have the courage to not only attain it, but see past those who are only here to feed on your bones. You may not walk on water, but you are still a miracle in these eyes that were once blind before you.

The water walks by us down below. It carries leaves, life, and anything with a spirit. It is the revival of all living things. This cathedral is not a church. It is a welcoming promise to never return you the same way you entered its doors. It is the eminence I am after. It is the only water that can cleanse the sins I consist of. It is my proof that angels and demons are made with the same wings. It is how I see my life finally coming out with a true victory.

Fall in love with anything you can. It is the most honest and beautiful thing you can do with your life. Give it all to the cosmos or nature or whatever seeks you out to bless you. You deserve it as much as anyone. I would tell you to be careful with it, but a wild horse will always need room to run, just as the wild in you will need adventure to be at home.

The weather right now is my ideal place of living. Low humidity, mid 70s, sunny, with a southern breeze. I could write for lifetimes with weather like this. I could write about nothing but how it makes me feel more than any single body ever could. My peace sits on this bench, staring out into nature and it reflecting its soul back to me.

The wind blows through my sorrows and comes back to me as wishful regrets. I had someone I loved more than myself. She will remain my greatest lesson and loss of my life. I know I still have years left on this earth, but when you lose someone like her, you miss out on the rest of your journey looking for her again in the places you keep her alive in.

We at times forget where we need to go and get consumed with the idea of it all. We must recall and remember who we are and what it feels like to be present where we are. Maybe there is something better somewhere else, but it will never be enough for the wandering attached to our bones, to the human side of our soul.

Life may never be as good as it is now with you beside me and my heart on the outside of my chest. I am now at a new stage where love means a new breath, a new movement entirely. You were always better for me than the moon herself. Your light fit my cracks, as if you were my best parts to begin with. My life began the night you separated my demons from their fight.

Nesting beneath my eyes, your hands hold onto what is left, what remains of me. I have wondered ever since I was a boy, what a life like yours could be like when pressed against me like midnight to the sun. You are the end of my pain. You are the sensation of early morning dew dripping from the grass and onto my soul. A newly found appreciation for love is what and who you are to me. My name never meant anything until you took the time to say it properly, with a defined defiance for grace. You are the greatest breath I have ever taken.

Leaning into you, I feel what it must be like to understand love. You are the magic between breaths, a solitude meant to be broken by sweetness. I am at times a walking contradiction. It is only when you are next to me do I know what living is and could be. I swear to whatever God is above us and whatever angel is below us, you are the gold and fire all mortals speak of when it comes to moonish things. I will never be able to love you right, but I will be right beside you when I try.

My knees are bent. My back is bending down to pick up what is left of a man you gave up on. I may never find who I was before you, but I will make it back to a beginning where you know how much better I am since you left me. My hands still hold the shape of you so well. I am learning how to speak again, how to rise again, how to raise my fists in hallelujahs. Who you are to me now is nothing more than a memory I hang on the wall to remind myself when in love, giving all you have, is still the most beautiful and bravest thing you can do in life.

Everyone I have wanted to be with, turned out to be with someone else or was married. My luck in finding love has been absent. My blindness towards love itself has led me to the darkest part of my life.

I always wondered what life would feel like once you found the kind, your kind. It feels like your favorite color played in a song and sung by your favorite artist dead or alive. For me, it feels like punching these keys. This is the closest to sex I have been in years. It is my favorite noise, even more so than your moans. I am good today. I am making love again.

Love only knows how to survive. Goodbye may find us, but the longing, aching, reaching, and lost attempts to speak, they stay. It always comes to us in waves. There's no regret with feeling. It is what separates souls and humans.

Some days I barely know if I am alive or not. All it takes is for you to say my name for me to know how my breathing is keeping you and I from failing. The sun jerks around, flowers perk up from their soft ground around the grave where she left me. You are all woman, all fire, and every bit of the love I need. I have yet to meet your body, but my entirety is already yours. I long for days and nights with you, when all we do is hold onto each other tighter, longer, everlasting.

There is no such thing as being close enough to you; my soul is in your bones. We have always been cosmic and out of place. We have always lived with hearts beating for the strangeness that completes us. We have always been gemstones and birth signs. We will remain our only form of natural and boundless formalities made from loss and a grief that birthed us to find the other. My sickness lies within you.

I would love to give you a place to rest your head and body after a day of adventuring. I think that is what scares me the most about getting into a relationship at this point in my life. The fact that everyone has an attention span of a maverick wave. We are always after something new once we get tired of or ruin the one thing we thought was irreplaceable.

We are the keepers of nothing,

I took my eyes out of my skull, placed them in the stars above me. I needed to know if it was about seeing beauty on the outside, on the flesh of a love you feel for someone. I needed to know if my eyes could actually hold your light, just as you have kept mine for all of these tender years.

I am in love with you, but as we are presently constructed, there is no room for either of us in the life of the other one. We are kept away from each other, like amber and the flame. If God and the devil knew how much I needed you right now, they would know my fight and fire would make their souls shake. I am not ready to give up on you yet, on us, on the memories waiting for us to remember. You are my tactile response as to why this heart of mine is fueled by wild notions of your body against mine, in this life and whatever awaits us as we remain cemented in time.

I am trying to get through this, through the graves and dead in my way. I am not common as some are. I am rickety, not well kept, deeply tortured by a love and war that has passed me by. I have yet to find someone willing to taste my words and love me as I do them. The ones who have tried, were only there for the show. Everyone wants to be loved, until the love they have longed for shows up and becomes more of a chore than habit. I do not understand humans for the most of the time. If love is so fucking rare and precious, why do we keep pushing away those who want to care for us? I believe we all have the capacity to love, but not all of us can withstand our own love in return. We want more, but only less is found.

In life, there will be a chance to get back everything you think you have lost. You can find it all in a song, memory, or a rest stop along the way. You are directed to these things based on what you give back, not what you get in return.

I look at you and know where I came from. Certain humans put off energies you feel based on where in this world you have gone and traveled. Love meets you at these locations. It is then you understand time and space a bit more.

There is something about feeling everything that makes you appreciate those who are in your life greater than ever before. Even with your heart beating out of your chest, they remain there, holding your hand through it all. Family takes on a whole new meaning when you have been lost your entire life. They never once asked you to come back home. They allow you to air out outside, until you reek of personal freedom.

I do not want to be remembered for a short story about what could have been or a simple quote protesting what love is or isn't. I want to be more than a few shallow words that can make you feel everything you have been keeping in or nothing at all. I want to skip my soul across these neon skies and arrive where few have had the guts to go. I want to break bread with strangers and lovers and those who never viewed themselves as anyone important. This year has already blessed me with a new perspective, a new earthly voice to speak with. It has given my mind the ability to find peace where she left me and where someone else may be able to love mer. I am obsessed with strange, with the extraordinary ability of how a heart can love even harder when it is in a pile of its own brokenness.

I have a love to give you, but you close your eyes when I tell you. I cannot make you believe in magic. I can only show you how it is created. I wish you would give me a chance. I guess my ache and yours remain indifferent, just as our love could never withstand this distance.

Maybe I am too tortured of a man, of a soul, for the angel in you. It was a sweet thought, an endearing and righteous calling thinking maybe I could be someone you wanted to love one day. I am all too familiar with the sound and tone of your voice now. I know goodbye will soon follow whatever falls from your next thought. I think life has me all wrong. I am not asking for the best love out there. I am demanding the best love for me moving forward. Some people may learn to love who I am, but they will never make it through to the ending, because safety and security is a language I do not speak until I know they have it for me. Goodbye comes in many forms. Yours was saying, "sorry," then me saying, "okay."

You became my first wish of the new year. I will call out your name each time I see one of my angel numbers. I may never be any closer to you than this, but you need to know how much of my breath is already yours. You need to know the home inside me, the one you had built before this life, misses you. I keep looking out its windows in hopes you are running back to me, to us. If it takes being alone with my demons and you with your new love, I shall wait out both heaven and hell to have you as you always have been to me; something holy and wholly only for me. My lord, my God, I am defeated by your beauty. I am nesting in a sunset until I can hold you and your glory.

Maybe all I will ever be is a man carrying a few hundred scars and a few more broken hearts inside of a body that embodies what it is like to die a few times for the things you actually love and long for. Maybe I am waiting for something that will never come, but I will be prepared for your arrival, for your starry nights to marry my personified darkness.

I still do not know how to hold you properly.

My hands are still getting used to touching

art, beauty, and a love like yours.

Take me down to the song of your soul. Give me one last kiss, one last touch, one last dance. My feet only know this mumbled earth below me. I am in need of your chaos to rattle these caged bones of mine.

I may never be more ready to fail, to prosper, to give my all to a love I can only write about for now. I was not given this ache. I worked and nearly killed myself for what it means to me to have someone like you to lay my body on the line for. I am too soft for my own good, but my bones have broken my fall a time or two after getting too close to a love not made for my blood.

Love me like this, from where you are. I am tired and alone, but not dead yet. I am lonely and reflecting, but not moving forward yet. There are miles to go before my hands find new earth to dig in, to play in, to place these seeds I have been keeping like sacred secrets. Give me a love like this, like all of the times you could have quit, but loved beyond your bones. My soul has your heart safely placed next to each seed I give back to the places that gave me something to write about.

Sit with me. Tell me a story of how you found me.

Tell me a story of the fight and urgency that came along

with your illustriousness. I am here, yours, enthralled

with golden ambers when you hold me.

When all of this is over, heaven will call out for your hand.

I will never let you go. Not even after our wings touch the sun.

I am yours in whatever life that can house two wild and forever

souls. I am yours through victory and defeat.

Kiss me slowly, with purpose and without regret. I am only yours forever if that is all you can handle. I will love you like there is no other day after this one. I will love you with a million kisses upon the wounds you tell me about. I will love you with a million embraces on the days you feel less like a human and more like a body.

Tell me it is okay. Tell me it will all work out in the end between humans and souls. I am no beggar, but my knees will kiss the promise you make to me.

Lovely thoughts embrace my strangeness. It is then I know the devil has died and its demons walked into the light; your eyes. Freedom never felt or looked like a human until you covered me up with your armor.

My life doesn't need anyone who questions why I am in their life. I need someone to see me, to love without fear, and to touch my scars when they begin to ache for my losses.

I am a man on a quest for a truth only I can come home to. What and who I am today, cannot hold anyone else with these arms made of stone and regret.

I am still looking back on the way we were, on the way your eyes looked at me when you felt lost or out of place during the day. You and the moon always had that in common on the bluest of days.

I promise to keep these hands on you for the rest of the time

we have on this earth. I will plant you the most beautiful

sunsets to grow with us.

You always had to struggle through life. Maybe that is why I love you as much as I do. To see your fight, gives me strength to keep breathing alongside you.

I am done giving myself to things, to feelings not belonging to me. I am done giving myself to those who have zero interest in returning it the same. I am too old for everything it seems.

A part of me will be a part of you until we are apart from this

distance and become parted and pardoned by the stars keeping

us this far and separated.

We cannot stop our hearts from breaking over a love we will never know. I awake each day without knowledge of victory nor defeat. I am simply balancing between survival and my own demise.

These hands have been what's saved my life. They still reach

out for you, as if you are here. Pain has never felt more

palpable than when they come up empty

without you, without grace.

The clouds gather in a long and friendly embosomed of

shadows and light. I keep my eyes directed towards their magic

as often as I can to find my footing with my own.

Catch me when you can. Keep me pressed against your truth,

beauty, and religion. My ache will forever be yours and

because of your absence.

The open road brings me more poetry than any lover ever could. Be it the trees, wind, or birds keeping the breeze free. There is something about this openness that keeps my heart falling for it, infinitely and brazenly.

The hearse drives down the road with a body no longer full of light. It is always a strange thing for me to see one on the road. Whether it is accompanied by death or not, it is a swift reminder of how far you actually go in the moments after life.

One day you will wonder about me and why I was the

one who should have let you go. Your life will never

be able to hold the love inside of me.

Take my hands and place them

where you need them.

Your hurt will become my words,

until your love becomes mine.

I overthink a lot of my life. I still worry about my past,

as if it was a curse, instead of the blessing I know it

can be. I can never be lyrically enough with

my words for things I cannot have.

We want to believe we matter, that we are important to those around us. We will do whatever we can to chop ourselves down to prove our worth. It is shameful what we do for attention of those who we know are not good for our own future. A momentary reflection would show us how deathly it can be when turning yourself into the devil just because they showed you their horns first.

My vices have kept me alive as much as they have killed me. Allowing something good to happen to me is not what I am used to. My teeth are finally getting fixed and corrected after going my entire existence without caring for them. It is time I do the same thing with my life as a whole.

There are certain humans walking amongst us wearing wings as light. The beauty lies within the very bones that make her wild. If you sit with her, you will hear stories of a past that never knew her well enough to love who she was. If you watch her speak, you will watch how birds fly south to find warmer earth. A life is nothing more than filling in time in-between two dates. She is doing more with hers than most will ever dream of. She is doing more than most who already have been alive longer than the sun shining on them. There is a subtleness about her energy. You can feel it a thousand miles away with a force of a soft hand resting on a heart's face. Be gentle with her existence. Something this precious has only ever been felt by the Gods themselves.

I have been trying to find a new way to connect what I have lost, with what I have learned. I guess when all I have known is loss, learning anything else doesn't make too much sense to me. My lessons are written all over my body. I take my cues from my scars, because they seem to be the only real thing about me. Connecting a broken heart to any other living thing is not love, and that is what I have learned thus far.

You are the love I am going to grow old writing about.

You are the secret I will keep safe for as long as

your light remains a permanent illumination

for every word my soul has yet to share.

Maybe this time you will stay gone. Maybe this time your ghost will simply be a reminder, instead of a haunting. I know you left for good. I do not blame you. There is not any room in my life for maybes anymore.

I took a lot of my life for granted.

I had family taking care of me long before I asked

for their help. They loved me when I hated everyone,

especially myself. Most of the time, I do not deserve them,

but they tell me and show me without fail, what it means to

love someone when love is the last thing you tell yourself.

I have always known you to be mighty above everything else. Your love comes to me, blessed and kissed, by a preciousness created from a God I am starting to believe in. Your existence ignites every miracle swimming through my goddamn veins.

There is a great power in the love for self. A power not everyone finds or has the courage to discover. Life is nothing more than finding your purpose and dying for it a little each day. It is what grants us control over our enemies. It is what prompts us to bleed and chase down every single thing we grow crazy for and go mad for. It takes a certain wild, a blessing of wings, to become someone others tell us not to be. There is a love for us if we choose to believe and see what is inside of us. Reverie to the cause. Grace in the pause. We are where we were meant to be. Some are okay with it. Others dig into their bones a bit further for a more profound and resounding truth written on the stars inside the flesh we carry.

It started when I was a kid. I would listen to my parents arguing, sometimes fighting, but it all happened back then. Most days it was normal to feel everything, every word, every curse, every hell one could imagine. I was raised in the seventh circle during a time when others celebrated birthdays and holidays with family. I would look at my mother and wonder how much hurt could live within a human. I would wonder what caused her to be that way. I would do the same with my father, though his outbursts never lasted as long. He was more of the teacher, but still the enforcer other times. My abilities and talents were raised and nurtured back then. I could feel energies of those around me. I could hear thoughts and emotions. I thought I was crazy when I was six. I was just born with a sickness, a longing, a curse I never wanted. I am thankful I do have it now. I am not always wright in my intuitional advances. Some of the time I couldn't be any more wrong about a situation. I am still learning how to trust it and when to act on it. My parents loved each other for longer than I have ever loved, but those last five years of them being together will always stick out to me. I have tried to be better at everything I do because of their failures, their shortcomings. I have failed miserably at being a man, human, brother, friend, and lover. I never shy away from that. I just hope my future will be able to balance out my past. Even the devil can teach you things that are important if you understand his pain. I feel like it is my purpose to understand all the pain I come into contact with, even more so when it is my own. If I cannot, then I do not wish to give that duty to anyone else. The love I have is for someone that wants to try or at least give me effort. Until then, I will happily do it on my own and in my own way.

I am after a wild I may never fully understand, but my wings keep me free from all the demons chasing what is left of me. Love looks my way for a second glance, for a rightful approach to my existence. It becomes a daunting breath to take when my lungs beg, borrow, and steal what they can. I am better now. A more relentless heart gets me to open my eyes and trust what they see. I am no longer blind to my beauty, my arrow, my ability to speak without hesitation. Love is there. Love is here, I swear. It is my sun, my moon, my single flower protruding into the night sky to speak a language I am still learning. My fight is on my shield. My life is a sword staring back at the devil. Love knows me, I swear. It is my greatest friend when all else leaves me. It is what keeps me breathing with a purpose. I am not what you think I am. I am as mighty as any muse. I am not you.

Take my hand and put it into ours. I have gone too long without your voice, your love, your glorified warmth.

Take my body and put it against yours. I have gone too long without your impression, your expression, your imprint on this cold body of mine. Live for me and you will live forever within these words I write about a darling musing I cannot live without.

There is a love out there and though I may be growing weary, I am able to stand and fight for what remains. Life may get the best of my intentions, but I am in full bloom, a full moon of a soul, of a thought, of a relentless pursuit of what my wild needs. There are times I am not worthy of such a place, of such sweet parting. There will always be a part of me wanting to escape, wanting to fly, wanting to leave everything including this body behind. I am a traveler. I am a wanderlust. Where the wind blows, it speaks deeply to my bones. Maybe in another lifetime will sit with me as a friend and share its secrets to me about longevity. For now, I am in love with, love. There is no replacement for the losses I have endured, but there is common ground to plant my feet and grow with the trees.

Let it be soft as rain. Let it grow from the pain inflicted by the student still learning love's name. I am a master of nothing, but I do know what it is like to lose everything for a cause, even your mind. Maybe next time it will stay longer than the devil did. Maybe next time it won't feel like the last particles of earth cascading down onto this shivered face of mine. I am brave, but it takes more than that if you are ever to come back from a broken heart.

I thought I knew what it was like falling in love for the first time with a soul you meet from a past life. Goodbye sounds the same regardless of what face it is said by. I am continually reminded how to leave what was never meant for you in the first place. Love is not through with me just yet. I met someone a few days ago who looks a lot like a reason to try again. She walked me down an untraveled path. It was there I gave her a flower, a color, that I named after her.

I lay here with head in hand. I regret nothing, but when I look back on my life, I can still feel your stillness, your absolute closeness. It is such a bizarre thing and feeling to be alive, but still sense the death of who you were to me. I can still smell the body of who you once were before.

As I walked back to find where I had left who I was, I smiled at you long enough to give myself the closure you never gave me. I am okay and doing better than before. I can open my eyes and not be blinded by images of you. I was taught in order to type the truth, you must sit down and bleed. My wrists have been cut before, so I will let my fingers cut the pages instead. I am free from you, now.

The sun shines on everything out here. A few passing clouds get in its way, but if you are alive and breathing, it will find you. It will make you believe in good things again. It is the cure, the medication needed for anything stopping you from finding yourself. I sit with it for as long as I can. It seems to be my only friend at times.

It has been aberrant to say the least being away like this. Some days I have missed sharing my words. Other days I have been content on letting the writing breath on its own. It is a delicate balance being a writer these days and not being what a writer was before social media. No one had access to you. I knew I was born in the wrong era. Being out there has only confirmed it for me. We must know when to save ourselves and our work before we turn into slaves who never realize it. You must break away from anything rendering you from being yourself. Even if you lose money, you cannot allow it to make you lose yourself.

As we go about our lives, love is the one thing we can never fully be prepared for; When it comes, when it leaves. We are prisoners to our own beliefs, to our own ideals. We hope to find it before we find anything else, including ourselves. There is so much to learn from it and its absence. We must be prepared either way. It is a wild thing without structure. It is a calming beauty full of winged prayers and lightning bolts, readying themselves to strike our bones and try to break us, but we must laugh. We must break it before it touches us with cruel thoughts and wishes. We are the masters of our own divine. Where our hearts go, we mustn't be blind to what it is we feel. Where there is love, there is a kindred response awaiting our return.

There is a quiet beauty in our brokenness. The kind that gives love despite not ever having enough for our own bodies. We give and give, until our souls become light. There is no reason for why we are this way. All we know is how to be love itself. At an early age, we were given this beautiful truth and promise. We were born with the sun and moon providing us love within our bones. We walk in darkness, unafraid of demons and devils. We have battled far greater enemies than those. We are the brave ones others look for and point at when life becomes lifeless, when feeling becomes an unstable choice for living. Wherever love is, we will be there with our swords and shields. We only know this religion, and it is the only thing we will give our lives for. Blood to blood. Ashes to ashes. We are the elements of life itself. We are the crown.

I do not know how not to give all I have for the one I am with.

Even if you cannot give me back in full what I give to you,

I will still care for you and adore you. My heart does not know

how to give half of anything, just as it will never be able to

relinquish what it keeps inside.

Come to me breathless, with less than you believe yourself to be. I will gather your wounds and show you a love you will never go without again. It is you, me, and the love we keep until the end.

Take my hand and put it into yours. I have gone too long without your love, your voice, your glorified warmth. Take my body and put it against yours. I have gone too long without your impression, your expression, your imprint on these cold bones of mine. Live for me and you will live forever within these words I write about a darling musing I cannot live without.

Take me to the edge of who you are. Allow me to jump into the version you love the most. Allow me to love the version you hate the most. You will never go lonely as long as you know me. You will never be without my energy and soul. They both have been yours since the day you smiled and I felt every goodbye give meaning to this fearless hello.

Hold me close and tell me I am good enough. Hold me tight and remind me I am not what my thoughts speak out loud. I am an overly sensitive creature at times. I feel too much or barely the bearing winds. I do not seek out validation from you. I come fully prepared and battle-tested. I know myself well enough to ask for help and embracement when I feel lonely tapping on my shoulder. I am a human of needs.

You tell me I am too accepting of you. I laugh because I feel the same way towards you. You have never blinked at my darkness. You have only moved closer to me and these bones of mine. Maybe we both deserve more than this, but I promise you, I have never felt as full as I do when you ask how my day was or I catch you glancing at my work, wondering what words will be for you today. Of course, I wish things were different and we could be together, but I have never known a beautiful thing in my life that was fair. It happened slowly, memorably, never rushed to fit into present time and day. We will get there. I wouldn't share the secrets I have kept safe inside my heart all this time with someone I didn't think would not be there in the end with me. You are the grateful beginning and glorious ending to a life made specifically for you. Our souls were matched long before our rage ignited the fire we consume daily without ever feeling the flames. This distance isn't ideal for either of us, but with what we feel for the other, I will gladly take this form of you over anyone who could give me more of what you think I deserve. I deserve you. That is all and everything I am worthy of. It is all I will accept.

Sacred, Secret, and Holy

www.ingramcontent.com/pod-product-compliance
Lightning Source LLC
Chambersburg PA
CBHW011151290426
44109CB00025B/2563